PLAY WITH THE PROS

Perform with recorded accompaniments by top professional musicians! The **Solo Trax**® book and CD will provice hours of entertaining and useful practice. Each song has a brief intro to establish the tempo and style. Be sure to "tune up" before you start. Listen and match the tuning notes so you'll blend nicely with the band. Remember, you're playing with the PROS!

ISBN 978-0-634-00606-7

Walt Disney Music Company
Wonderland Music Company, Inc.

DISTRIBUTED BY

HAL•LEONARD® CORPORATION

7777 W. BLUEMOUND RD. P.O. BOX 13819 MILWAUKEE, WI 53213

Visit Hal Leonard Online at
www.halleonard.com

NOTES YOU NEED TO KNOW

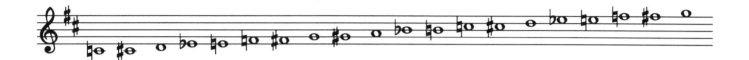

TIME VALUES YOU NEED TO KNOW

MICKEY MOUSE MARCH

Clarinet

Words and Music by
JIMMIE DODD

SUPERCALIFRAGILISTICEXPIALIDOCIOUS

(From Walt Disney's "MARY POPPINS")

Clarinet

Words and Music by
RICHARD M. SHERMAN and ROBERT B. SHERMAN

CHIM CHIM CHER-EE
(From Walt Disney's "MARY POPPINS")

Clarinet

Words and Music by
RICHARD M. SHERMAN and ROBERT B. SHERMAN

rit.

A DREAM IS A WISH YOUR HEART MAKES

(From Walt Disney's "CINDERELLA")

Clarinet

Words and Music by MACK DAVID,
AL HOFFMAN and JERRY LIVINGSTON

Moderato

A SPOONFUL OF SUGAR

Clarinet

Words and Music by
RICHARD M. SHERMAN and ROBERT B. SHERMAN

WINNIE THE POOH

Clarinet

Words and Music by
RICHARD M. SHERMAN and ROBERT B. SHERMAN

ZIP-A-DEE-DOO-DAH

Clarinet

Words by RAY GILBERT
Music by ALLIE WRUBEL

THE WORK SONG

Clarinet

Words and Music by MACK DAVID,
AL HOFFMAN and JERRY LIVINGSTON

CANDLE ON THE WATER
(From Walt Disney Productions "PETE'S DRAGON")

Clarinet

Words and Music by
AL KASHA and JOEL HIRSCHHORN

Spiritually

BIBBIDI-BOBBIDI-BOO

(From Walt Disney's "CINDERELLA")

Words by JERRY LIVINGSTON
Music by MACK DAVID and AL HOFFMAN

Clarinet

Brightly (In Two)

LET'S GO FLY A KITE

Clarinet

Words and Music by
RICHARD M. SHERMAN and ROBERT B. SHERMAN

TOYLAND MARCH

Clarinet

Words by MEL LEVEN
Music by GEORGE BRUNS
(Adapt. From V. Herbert Melody)

March Tempo

IT'S A SMALL WORLD
(Theme From the Disneyland and Walt Disney World Attraction, "IT'S A SMALL WORLD")

Clarinet

Words and Music by
RICHARD M. SHERMAN and ROBERT B. SHERMAN